LIVE AND LEARN
AND PASS IT ON

Volume III

~~~

*People ages 5 to 95 share what they've discovered
about life, love, and other good stuff*

Written and compiled by H. JACKSON BROWN, JR.

RUTLEDGE HILL PRESS®

Nashville, Tennessee

A Thomas Nelson Company

Published by Rutledge Hill Press, a Thomas Nelson Company, P.O. Box 141000, Nashville, Tennessee
37214.

Typography by D&T/Bailey Typesetting, Inc., Nashville, Tennessee.

Library of Congress Cataloging-in-Publication Data

Live and learn and pass it on : people ages 7 to 92 share what they've learned about life, love, and
other good stuff / written and compiled by H. Jackson Brown, Jr.
p. cm.
ISBN 1-55853-840-2 (v. 3)
1. Life cycle, Human—Miscellanea. 2. Developmental psychology—Miscellanea. 3. Maturation
(Psychology)—Miscellanea. I. Brown, H. Jackson, 1940- .
HQ799.95.L55 1991   91-32132
158'.1—dc20   CIP

Printed in the United States of America
1 2 3 4 5 6 7 8 9 — 05 04 03 02 01 00

Introduction

Encouraged by my invitation in the two previous volumes of *Live and Learn and Pass It On,* thousands of readers have written to me to share a lesson or two about what they've learned about life. And what a pleasure it is to read them. Upon discovering an unusually perceptive observation or witty suggestion, I feel like a carpenter who has received a gift of a sharp new saw or a well-balanced hammer. We all know the pleasure of working with new tools, whether we're building a bookcase or a life.

The contributors to this book are all ages and from every economic and social background. They would not consider themselves philosophers or gurus. And yet here, in a short sentence or two, they offer us worlds of wisdom.

Oh, how I would like to meet each one personally—to pull up a chair at their kitchen table and linger over a cup of coffee—or maybe take them for a ride in the country in a covertible with the top down. I long to know more about them. I want to hear about their successes and setbacks, their dreams and disappointments; what they've learned to live with and what they've learned to live without.

As you read these observations, you will get a glimpse now and then of lonely hearts and lost hopes. But overall, what comes through is a sense of cheerfulness, resolve, and the importance of keeping things in perspective. A forty-two-year-old father writes, "I've learned that a shoeshine box made by my eight-year-old son at Vacation Bible School is my most prized possession." That's as powerful a statement as you will ever read about priorities and what makes life worth living.

The seventeenth-century English clergyman Thomas Fuller wrote, "If you have knowledge, let others light their candle at it." Thanks to these 302 people who have shared their "life's lessons" with me, my candle now burns with a lively flame. I invite you to light yours from mine. By holding them together, we'll light our own path as well as signal a direction for those who follow.

H.J.B.
Tall Pine Lodge
Fernvale, Tennessee

Acknowledgments

MY GRATEFUL THANKS to all who contributed to this collection of discoveries and insights: Anna Abraham, Janie Adams, DeAnn Adelman, Silvia Alba, Mary Allen, Diane Amadruto, Katarina Arguinzoni, Jeff Arney, Janice Austin, Bree Barton, Eileen Bassirl, Corinne Belsky, Jessica Berg, Rolanda Bertz, Jessica Bette, Laura Bogdas, Annie Borger, Linda Boyd, Joanne Bozue, Bill Brabbin, Alda Bradkoski, Carol Brandes, Antonio Bravo, Florence Brewis, Jasper Brewster, Dolores Brough, Betty Brown, Amy Brown, Jennifer Bruce, Mary Brunson, Marissa Bucci, Kay Burger, Therese Burke, Pat Bush, Elsa Campbell, Tom Candalino, Gerry Cantrell, Bea Carmody, Mel Cason, Megan Cassidy, Louise Cherry, Courtney Christopher, Sherry Cleaves, Shirley Clyburn, Michael Comprola, Joseph Connelly, Marie Cook, Suzanne Cook-Riddle, Christi Cotham, John Crawford, Brenda Crawley, Michelle Creason, Ann Crews, Timothy Cuff, Cali Cunningham, Alex Curio, Mary Cuthbert, Kathy Dalton, Nicole Darling, Angela Davies, Anne Davis, Sally Davis, Delbert Davis, David Debter, Lawrence Dikeman, Cathleen Donovan, Jennifer Draksler, Norma Duckett, Ruby Edwards, Don Eisenberg, Mary Elliott, Lorraine Failla, Melissa Ferrarese, Amie Fiedler, Virginia FitzSimmons, Sylvia Flowers, Darcy Fournier, Robert Fox, Rob Foxworthy, Carolyn Freeman, Corissa Frericks, Janelle Froelich, Christine Gardner, Ildiko Gaspar, William Gates, Jeannie George, Sam Goldsmith, Michelle Gomez, Dawn Goodrich, Mary Grabowski, Kara Green, Dennis Guadalupe, Renee Haines, Sylvia Hamilton, Alice Haney, Catherine Hardy, Walt Harper, Jeffrey Harrington, Dennis Harrington, Rita Harris, Holly Haukaas, Lois Hausner, Lisa Hay, Dorothy Hella, Krystal Henagan, Brenda Henry, Heidi Hildebrand, Chrystal Hinz, Bill Hockaday, Jane Holding, Berdyne Hoover, Kathleen Howell, Jacqueline Hudnell, Nikia Huffman, Jake Hughes, Scott Hummer, Holly Hutchins, Jennifer Johnson, Laurie Johnson, Lori Johnson, Lindsey Johnson, Ann Jolliffe, Wesley Jones, Courtney Judd, Michael Julien, Karen Karp, Lindsay Katal, A. Katin, Jenne Keller, Sandy Kenslow, Mark Kern, Shawn Kerstetter, Fatimah Khan, Kathryn Kiebler, Chelsey Knauer, Judith Kopec, Paul Kostansek, Susan Kratzenberg, Kristen Krugeinhard, Tracy Kundinger, Brenda Laird, Eden Langewis, Christopher Lawless, Evelina Lawrence, Angela Lechter, Rachel Lee, Alison Lipari, Lori Lipton, Robert Lott, Patricia Lukoschek, Wanda Lynn, Lynn Madden, Suzanne Mailloux, Jana Marine, Glenn Martin,

Marion Martin, Meaghan Martin, Angela Maschari, Terry Masek, Shelley Mason, Kevin Masser, Katherine Massey, Marco Matute, Susan Mayer, Leah Mazar, Joseph McCue, Patrick McGlashan, Brant McKeever, Chalonne McLeod, Rebecca McMichael, Alline McNeil, Franklyn McWay, Sherry Meadows, Megan Meeker, Imy Menser, Kimberley Mentes, Alexis Michael, M.A. Moldenhauer, Sherwood Moran, Maureen Mosley, Julia Mullane, Phyllis Muller, Hilary Munn, Jennifer Murfin, Jill Murphy, Michelle Murphy, Kathy Nadason, Becky Newcomb, Ema Newcomb, Titi Nguyen, Kristina O'Brien, Misty O'Dell, Tess Oakes, Shelby Oberstein, Deborah Obrecht, Robin Osborne, Jamie Osman, Susan Osso, Kelley Paige, Ann Pate, Kimberly Peek, Candy Penner, Michelle Pennock, Wendy Pierret, Grace Piper, Kris Placencia, Claire Pocock, Sharon Popovich, Tom Porter, Laura Poulson, Chris Proffitt, Kaye Prouty, Vanessa Ray, Cynthia Read, Brian Rees, Jenny Rehbein, Cindy Reisinger, Liz Rice, Erika Rickard, Jennifer Ristic, Lynn Robards, Brian Robinson, Celeste Rodriguez, Brenda Roe, Chris Rogers, Patti Rosenswie, Tamara Ross, Carrie Rossetti, Spencer Royer Jr., Sheri Sarsfield, Steve Saunders, June Sawyer, James (Sam) Sawyer, Lacie Saxton, Amy Schaffer, Nora Schill, Carrol Schroyer, Janie Schuelka, Justin Seibel, Elise Selinger, Kevin Shaffer, Carla Shasteen, Ruby Shine, Stephanie Sicoia, Steve Siglar, Shannon Skroback, Dana Slocomb, Kerry Smith, Terri Smith, Lindsay Smith, Susan Soderquist, Kat Sproule, Lucille St. Pierre, Cecilia Stamas, Edwin Steinsapir, Jaime Stoddard, Elizabeth Stone, Leta Stratton, Brenda Streatch, Susan Stulen, Maria Stutzman, Teresa Summerville, Michelle Sumovich, Kara Svendsen, Angela Swann, Kelly Taney, Stephani Tennant, Ashley Thomas, David Thomas, Kris Thommesen, Janice Thompson, Betty Trimm, Ann Troy, Heather Tygrett, Joyce Van Deusen, Hollie Van Kirk, Karla Venis, Catherine Vodrey, Stephanie Vosmus, Lisa Vrana, Elizabeth Vukovitch, David Wacker, Janet Wasilewski, Libby Waterbury, Shirley Watts, Lori West, Carol Whiteley, Bobbie Whitlock, Eric Wicktor, Stefanie Wielkopolan, Cynthia Williams, Eva Williams, Claudia Wineke, Kari Winter, Availl Woodward, Wayne Wyler, Janet Yeakley, Danielle Zarda, Hilary Zetlin, Molly Ziebell, and Catalina Zobel.

Books by H. Jackson Brown, Jr.

I've learned that you realize you have locked the keys in your car the instant you slam the door shut.

—*Age 44*

I've learned that you should never attempt putting on a brand new pair of support hose in 90-degree weather after taking a shower.

—*Age 39*

I've learned that if I had listened to Mom, I would have avoided 90 percent of life's problems.

—*Age 20*

I've learned that if you're going to pray about
something, why worry? If you're going to worry,
why pray?

—Age 70

I've learned that a hug from my husband sends his
strength into my body.

—Age 39

I've learned that children do not want anything
until after you have poured milk on your cereal.

—Age 19

I've learned that you should never let your wildest, craziest friend put her hand on the back of your head in front of a whipped cream cake. —*Age 8*

I've learned that the small garden tools I can't find will be in plain sight as soon as I purchase new ones. —*Age 63*

I've learned that I've never regretted doing extra work. —*Age 17*

I've learned that if you have something, material or physical, that gets broken, lost, or damaged, if it can be repaired, replaced, or healed, then you have nothing to worry about.
—Age 74

I've learned that the best gift to give or receive is a book that touches the heart.
—Age 25

I've learned that red towels never stop fading.
—Age 46

I've learned I should never pinch my husband's nostrils together while he's snoring.
                                                                    —*Age 40*

I've learned that you shouldn't choose a roommate who comes to look at the place with her boyfriend.
                                                                    —*Age 23*

I've learned that a creative mess is preferable to idle neatness.
                                                                    —*Age 85*

I've learned that wives don't want advice, they
mostly just want to be held.   *—Age 32*

I've learned that when my neighbor's children
come over for the day, it makes me appreciate
mine all the more.   *—Age 25*

I've learned that you should never park your new
car beside a beat-up car in the parking lot.   *—Age 72*

I've learned that there's more to life than keeping everything you own, including your person, looking like it's never been used.

—*Age 50*

I've learned that you should get a puppy before you decide to have children.

—*Age 28*

I've learned that my dad likes to get those sweet, mushy greeting cards as much as my mom does.

—*Age 26*

I've learned that even with the lights out, I can still find the cashews in the mixed nuts.

—Age 50

I've learned that while you hated nap time in preschool, you would love for your manager to hand you a blanket, a pillow, and a glass of Kool-Aid at work.
—*Age 24*

I've learned the great value of the three Fs: forgive, forget, and forge ahead.
—*Age 47*

I've learned that I should always laugh at my dad's jokes no matter how lame they are.
—*Age 13*

I've learned that a good way to save money is to be too busy to go shopping.

—Age 88

I've learned that when my husband misplaces one of his belongings, he expects me to know exactly where he left it.

—Age 24

I've learned that you should never use safety pins while changing a baby's diaper on a waterbed.

—Age 26

I've learned that you should never tell your little brother that you're not going to do what your mom told you to do.

—*Age 12*

I've learned that you should never hit a pile of dog-do with a weed whacker.

—*Age 39*

I've learned that it's okay to feel sorry for yourself; just don't let it last for more than five minutes.

—*Age 57*

I've learned that when my son is pitching, they all look like strikes to me. —*Age 34*

I've learned that to stay away from a previous argument, you need to stay away from the person you're having the argument with. —*Age 18*

I've learned that mothers don't always know best. Sometimes they're learning as they go along. —*Age 14*

I've learned that you should never eat the cafeteria food when it looks like it's moving.   —*Age 12*

I've learned that the better the doctor, the harder it is to read his or her handwriting.   —*Age 51*

I've learned that when my older sister says that she'll be out of the bathroom in five minutes, I should just sit down and start reading *War and Peace*.   —*Age 14*

I've learned that what I call clean, my mom calls messy.

—Age 11

I've learned that a bottle of catsup should be on the table three times a day if there is a child in the house.

—Age 60

I've learned that there is nothing better than to sit in the straw and hold a new foal's head in my lap.

—Age 15

I've learned
that when
you've pushed
yourself as far
as you think
you can go, you
can always go
just a little bit
further.

—Age 23

I've learned that the only time you're guaranteed not to get something you want is when you don't try for it. —Age 13

I've learned that no matter how small the kitchen, never buy a table with only two chairs. —Age 42

I've learned that it's best not to discuss how many children I want to have while my wife is pregnant.

—Age 41

I've learned that when you are away at college, you
check the mailbox at least twice a day.   —*Age 18*

I've learned that when you tell your younger
brother that he can fly, he'll try it.   —*Age 12*

I've learned that the day the bill that you don't
want your husband to see arrives is the day he goes
to the mailbox first.   —*Age 32*

I've learned that nothing smells as good as my
boyfriend's favorite sweater.   *—Age 19*

I've learned that you shouldn't ask for anything
that costs more than five dollars when your
parents are doing taxes.   *—Age 9*

I've learned that people have no interest in going
into a room until they see that the door is shut.

—Age 23

I've learned that having someone tell you he loves you and having someone show you he loves you are two completely different things. *—Age 18*

I've learned that biscuits will not brown until you walk away from the oven; then they burn. *—Age 19*

I've learned that after your daughter borrows your car, the radio dials are never where you set them.

—Age 47

I've learned that it takes years to build up trust and only seconds to destroy it. —Age 15

I've learned that when I cook using my grandma's recipes, my kitchen smells as good as hers. —Age 27

I've learned that the side of the milk carton that says "Open Here" is harder to open than the other side. —Age 54

I've learned that the best weight-loss program is a broken heart.
—*Age 24*

I've learned that you should never try to push a pig around that is bigger than you are.
—*Age 11*

I've learned that I can't dust the table with the photo albums on it without stopping to look at the pictures.
—*Age 42*

I've learned that when I am feeling terribly unloved by someone, I need to ask myself what I've done recently to show I love them.   —*Age 29*

I've learned that you should never be sarcastic with police officers.   —*Age 43*

I've learned that you shouldn't hold a baby above your head after he has eaten.   —*Age 14*

I've learned that being a teenager is as hard on your parents as it is on you.

—*Age 13*

I've learned that working in a garden at sunrise has a tremendous effect on the soul. —Age 32

I've learned that when you're at a family picnic, you shouldn't say you don't like what you're eating because the person sitting next to you might have prepared it. —Age 18

I've learned that my wife contributes to everything I do simply by being there. —Age 53

I've learned that we don't have to change friends if we understand that friends change.

—*Age 16*

I've learned that I shouldn't call my identical twin sister ugly.

—*Age 12*

I've learned that no matter how many expensive toys you lavish on your cats, they still prefer empty paper sacks.

—*Age 24*

I've learned that when a father takes a son fishing, the least important thing to either one is whether they catch any fish.
                                                    —Age 22

I've learned that every woman is beautiful when she smiles.
                                                    —Age 66

I've learned that it's not a good idea to try to break in a new bra during a transcontinental flight.
                                                    —Age 46

I've learned that I know I am growing old when my ballpoint pens are inscribed with the names of companies now defunct. —*Age 71*

I've learned that falling snow is the prettiest when seen through the sunroof of a moving car. —*Age 15*

I've learned that I shouldn't inhale through my nose when I'm eating a powdered doughnut.

—*Age 51*

I've learned that you should never try to ride your bicycle over a basketball. —*Age 14*

I've learned that I should never write anything in my diary that I wouldn't want someone to read, and that I shouldn't do anything that I wouldn't write in my diary. —*Age 21*

I've learned that it is okay to give advice but you shouldn't expect anyone to take it. —*Age 86*

I've learned that when you buy a car for the first time, your number of friends increases dramatically.
—*Age 16*

I've learned that a daughter is never too old to hug and kiss her father in public.
—*Age 25*

I've learned that you should never underestimate a child's ability to get into more trouble.
—*Age 15*

I've learned that broken cookies have fewer calories.

—Age 82

I've learned that I should listen carefully to any advice my grandparents offer. It is the most valuable advice I can get.

—Age 20

I've learned that if my best friend doesn't like my boyfriend, I should look for a new boyfriend.

—Age 20

I've learned that the biggest regrets in life are the risks that you didn't take.
—*Age 14*

I've learned that a funny hat can change your attitude.
—*Age 22*

I've learned that as you grow older, everything seems to settle south. Sometimes you are lucky enough to have it be your address as well.
—*Age 39*

I've learned that sometimes just taking a nap can be the best medicine.

—*Age 18*

I've learned that men who wear boxer shorts are more fun.
                                                    —*Age 21*

I've learned that you shouldn't cry over anything that can't cry back.
                                                    —*Age 60*

I've learned that you should never leave your one-year-old Dalmatian alone in a room with a black permanent marker and real clean carpet.   —*Age 11*

I've learned that you should never date a man who is prettier than you are.
—*Age 31*

I've learned that it's easier to be patient with my granddaughter than it was with my own daughters when they were her age.
—*Age 53*

I've learned that cereal always tastes better from the little snack boxes.
—*Age 29*

I've learned that as soon as I've cleaned up the kitchen, someone says they're hungry. *—Age 62*

I've learned that my mom was right. All those popular, promiscuous girls with the groovy clothes did amount to nothing. *—Age 38*

I've learned that maybe someday I'll be as perfect as I say I am when I fill out a job application.

—Age 20

I've learned that a 6.8 earthquake makes all your other problems seem trivial. —*Age 28*

I've learned that fourteen-year-old sisters take literally a recipe that says "mix by hand." —*Age 18*

I've learned that someone who has never said "I'm sorry" after a five-year relationship is not someone I want to spend the rest of my life with. —*Age 22*

I've learned that if you say "I love you" to your
parents, they're going to ask you, "What do you
want?"
—*Age 13*

I've learned that you don't really know a person
until you've made them mad.
—*Age 22*

*I've learned that happiness is not how much you have
but your capacity to enjoy what you have.*
—*Age 44*

I've learned that the older I get, the more I say "I don't know." When I was younger, I thought I knew it all.
—*Age 65*

I've learned that wearing anything too small is a sure way to ruin my day.
—*Age 44*

I've learned that a great personality can make someone seem to grow more attractive every day.
—*Age 20*

I've learned that no matter how anxious I may seem to send my kids off to school in the morning, nothing makes me happier than seeing them come home in the afternoon.   —*Age 42*

I've learned that to enjoy time alone, you must first appreciate the person you are with.   —*Age 51*

I've learned that your dog lives with you, but you live with your cat.   —*Age 49*

I've learned that the worst thing in life to be without is love, but toilet paper comes in a close second.

—*Age 59*

I've learned that you can live with choices you have made yourself, but you live to regret the choices you let others make for you.

—*Age 29*

I've learned that it is impossible to win an argument with a six-year-old.

—*Age 18*

I've learned that to find the best places in a town to eat, ask a fireman or policeman.

—*Age 34*

I've learned that some folks are like the bottom half of a fraction—the bigger they try to be, the smaller they really are.

—*Age 60*

I've learned that child-proof bottles of medicine are sometimes adult-proof, too.

—*Age 55*

I've learned that you have to reach for the stars. They're not just going to land on your front porch.

—*Age 15*

I've learned that if I think of my husband's snoring as a happy cat purring, I can handle it better for a little while.

—Age 34

I've learned that the more you're in a hurry, the longer it takes to get your locker open.

—Age 13

I've learned that the sweetest sound of all is my own name spoken by a boy I care about.

—Age 18

I've learned that if someone asks "How are you doing?" it's not necessary to give them a full health report.
—Age 65

I've learned that when you go to the dentist, it pays if you've brushed your teeth.
—Age 11

I've learned that if you want an immediate high, give a homeless person ten dollars.
—Age 32

I've learned that when I'm angry, my mouth works faster than my brain.

—Age 58

I've learned that grandparents can be just as much of a joy to their grandchildren as their grandchildren are to them.

—Age 18

I've learned that in relationships, it's better to have an end with misery than misery without an end.

—Age 43

I've learned that after you retire, you spend half your time looking for things you lose. —*Age 74*

I've learned that making sure my best friend is happy is as important as making sure that I'm happy. —*Age 19*

I've learned that there is no feeling quite so nice as your child's hand in yours. —*Age 37*

I've learned that a shoeshine box made by my eight-year-old son at Vacation Bible School is my most prized possession. —Age 42

I've learned that when you're in love, you always have something to talk about. —Age 20

I've learned that if you have a job without any problems, you don't have much of a job. —Age 35

I've learned that if you spend your life always looking forward to something else, the present just slips away.   —*Age 16*

I've learned that everyone has two choices — either you grow up and take responsibility for your life or you don't.   —*Age 51*

I've learned that good cooks never lack friends. —*Age 42*

I've learned that living alone after an unhappy
marriage is heaven.
                                                    —*Age 80*

I've learned as a sixth grade teacher that when I
send more than two boys to the restroom at a
time, the principal usually ends up bringing them
back.
                                                    —*Age 34*

I've learned that I want to exercise, but not now.
                                                    —*Age 54*

I've learned that anger is an ill wind that blows out
the lamp of reason.   —*Age 76*

I've learned that no matter how old I get, I like my
mom taking care of me when I'm sick.   —*Age 25*

I've learned that you should never mention ice
cream when you're baby-sitting if you're not sure
there's some in the refrigerator.   —*Age 11*

I've learned that you can't raise your family or run a business by remote control. —*Age 45*

I've learned that the only thing you can be sure of improving is yourself. —*Age 61*

I've learned that you get the best feeling when you return home after a long absence and see that everything is just the same as when you left. —*Age 20*

I've learned that bragging on your children is one of life's greatest pleasures.

—Age 32

I've learned that work is when you sweat and you don't want to. Leisure is when you sweat and you don't care.

—*Age 55*

I've learned that there is no advertising as effective as something recommended by a friend.

—*Age 39*

I've learned that you can tell a lot about a person by looking in the trunk of his or her car.

—*Age 50*

I've learned that the gauge of success is not whether you have a tough problem, but whether it's the same problem you had last year. —*Age 49*

I've learned that the more content I am with myself, the fewer material things I need. —*Age 36*

I've learned that the most endearing three little words I can say to my wife are, "Let's eat out."

—*Age 71*

I've learned that you lose only the expensive sunglasses and pens. The cheap ones are always around.

—*Age 32*

I've learned that the word "oops" is not in God's vocabulary.

—*Age 32*

I've learned that the wealthiest of women is she whose daughter grows up to be her best friend.

—*Age 74*

I've learned that if you have a loving family, it's
amazing what you can do without.   —*Age 39*

I've learned that when you begin to ask yourself if
it's your fault, it usually is.   —*Age 20*

I've learned that every time I call someone that I
haven't spoken to in a long time, they say, "I was
just going to call you."   —*Age 33*

I've learned that watching a child learn to read is as exciting as watching him learn to walk. —*Age 39*

I've learned that it's better to hear from your children and grandchildren when they want something than never to hear from them at all. —*Age 60*

I've learned that those who ask "Can you keep a secret?" can't. —*Age 78*

I've learned that no one was put here to be in charge of making me happy. That's my job. —*Age 42*

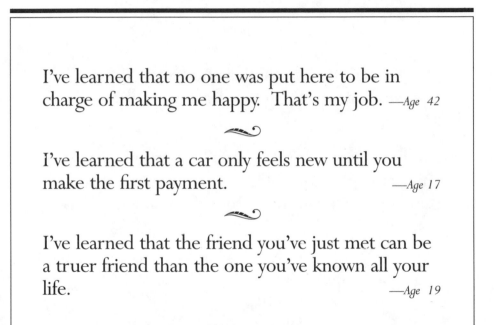

I've learned that a car only feels new until you make the first payment.   —*Age 17*

I've learned that the friend you've just met can be a truer friend than the one you've known all your life.   —*Age 19*

I've learned that you should never pull a loose
tooth with tweezers.   —*Age 8*

I've learned that I cry each time I watch the movie
Father of the Bride.   —*Age 38*

I've learned that a well-reared child results in
rewarding grandchildren, even to the fourth
generation.   —*Age 85*

I've learned that the easiest way to get grounded is to interrupt my mother during *Seinfeld.*   —*Age 17*

I've learned that I can never go to Wal-Mart and buy just one thing.   —*Age 24*

I've learned that breaking rules always has consequences, especially when you've broken your own rules.   —*Age 16*

I've learned that we are judged by what we finish, not by what we start.
—*Age 62*

I've learned that no matter how many tears and sleepless nights you've experienced, if you can walk away from a relationship cherishing more than you regret, it was not a waste of time. —*Age 26*

I've learned that good advice is no better than poor advice unless you take it.
—*Age 58*

I've learned that a woman who can potty-train triplets can do anything.

—Age 29

I've learned that the older my parents get, the
sweeter their voices sound. —*Age 34*

I've learned that the smell of a dentist's office gives
me a headache. —*Age 15*

I've learned that change is a challenge for the
courageous, an opportunity for the alert, and a
threat to the insecure. —*Age 87*

I've learned that big problems are no match for big, brave hearts.
—*Age 57*

I've learned that words are the most powerful weapon in the world and should be used with extreme caution.
—*Age 52*

I've learned that nothing tastes as sweet as a kiss from a child who's just sucked on a lollipop.

—*Age 29*

I've learned that the more respect I give my parents, the more respect they give me.   —*Age 17*

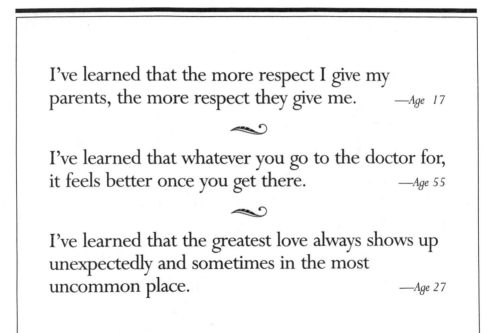

I've learned that whatever you go to the doctor for, it feels better once you get there.   —*Age 55*

I've learned that the greatest love always shows up unexpectedly and sometimes in the most uncommon place.   —*Age 27*

I've learned that my cat purrs loudest when he's lying on the book I'm trying to read. —*Age 22*

I've learned that no matter how much work a husband does around the house, if he doesn't know how to give his wife affection, the marriage can go down the drain. —*Age 46*

I've learned that will power is the ultimate power.

—*Age 16*

I've learned that if you don't expect a thank-you,
giving is easy. —*Age 47*

I've learned that the best therapy in the world is
driving my convertible on a sunny day with no
destination in mind. —*Age 25*

I've learned that you can miss a lot of good things
in life by having the wrong attitude. —*Age 82*

I've learned that the day you begin a diet, someone wants to take you to dinner in your favorite restaurant. —*Age 24*

I've learned that I'm thankful for my parents' boundaries and rules. —*Age 13*

I've learned that you never outgrow the enjoyment of browsing in the toy department. —*Age 61*

I've learned that when your mom says "We'll talk about it later," the answer really is no. —*Age 7*

I've learned that your best friend is the person who comes to your dance recitals and names goldfish after you. —*Age 14*

I've learned that nothing is quite as good as the first scoop of peanut butter out of a new jar. —*Age 34*

I've learned that if you enjoy being a guest, you must sometimes be a host.   —*Age 41*

I've learned that if the one you're with doesn't make you a better and stronger person, you're with the wrong person.   —*Age 25*

I've learned that you should never let a day pass without telling your wife you love her.   —*Age 61*

I've learned that you should never give your wife an ironing board for Christmas even if she says she needs a new one.

—Age 39

I've learned that you should be careful when sitting down in a chair on rollers.

—Age 72

I've learned that you can make anyone smile if you give them a box of crayons and a coloring book.

—Age 21

I've learned that you should never walk on ice with your hands in your pockets.

—Age 12

I've learned that there is a big difference between two cloves of garlic and two bulbs of garlic. —*Age 37*

I've learned that people tend to rise to accomplishments they thought were beyond them if you show them by your confidence that they can do it. —*Age 53*

I've learned that if you tell a girl you love her, she will hit you. —*Age 10*

I've learned that because I have four children, aged 19, 16, 13, and 8, there is no real purpose for the snap on my wallet.
—Age 42

I've learned that pizza is good for breakfast, lunch, and dinner.
—Age 22

I've learned that it's discouraging to go swimsuit shopping with someone who wears a size three.

—Age 17

I've learned that it's embarrassing to have a glamour photograph made of yourself and not have anyone recognize that it's you.   —*Age 43*

I've learned that when your grandma says your feet smell a little, they really stink.   —*Age 12*

I've learned that anything that lasts only a short time is not worth making lifetime sacrifices for.

—*Age 25*

I've learned that if you don't want to forget something, stick it in your underwear drawer. —*Age 18*

I've learned that reading my son's favorite storybook to my grandson is a very pleasurable experience. —*Age 62*

I've learned that you shouldn't be so eager to find out a secret. It could change your life forever.

—*Age 31*

I've learned that doing volunteer work is one way for me to repay life for all of the wonderful things that I've been given.

—*Age 38*

I've learned that when my response to rudeness is kindness, I feel better.

—*Age 62*

I've learned that men don't do laundry because washing machines don't have remote controls.

—*Age 75*

I've learned that good habits are the shortest route to the top.
—Age 41

I've learned that at age 25 you're finding yourself, at age 45 you know yourself, and at age 65 you can be yourself.
—Age 68

I've learned that whenever I leave home without any make-up on, I'll run into my ex-boyfriend.

—Age 26

I've learned
that time spent
with your kids
pays lifetime
dividends.

—Age 61

I've learned that you shouldn't let anyone apologize to you through a closed door.

—Age 15

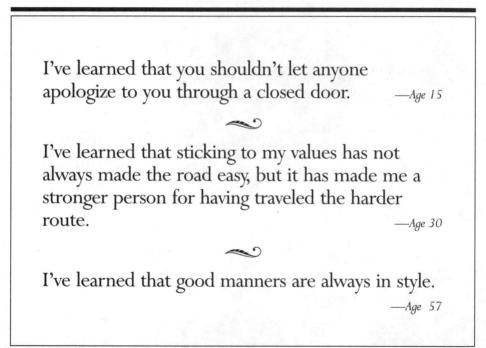

I've learned that sticking to my values has not always made the road easy, but it has made me a stronger person for having traveled the harder route.

—Age 30

I've learned that good manners are always in style.

—Age 57

I've learned that no matter where I go or where I visit, my favorite place in the whole world is my room.
—*Age 15*

I've learned that the only surprise a box of cereal holds these days is the price.
—*Age 46*

I've learned that when my dad and I jog together, it strengthens our relationship with each other as well as our bodies.
—*Age 18*

I've learned that about the only time my boss will return my phone calls is five minutes before I arrive in the morning, five minutes after I leave in the evening, or when I've gone to lunch.   —*Age 38*

I've learned that a diet is the penalty we pay for exceeding the food limit.   —*Age 76*

I've learned that when your teenager says, "I hate you," respond by saying, "I love you."   —*Age 44*

I've learned that I can't attend my child's school performance without a tissue in hand.   —*Age 29*

I've learned that I know I've had a great day if I come home and my clothes are dirty.   —*Age 19*

I've learned that saying "forgive me" is not the hardest thing for some people to say. Saying "you are forgiven" seems to be more difficult.   —*Age 70*

I've learned that you should be grateful for all you have, even if it isn't enough.
—*Age 42*

I've learned that the clothes I like best are the ones with the most holes in them.
—*Age 26*

I've learned that no matter how much you fight with your siblings during childhood, they grow up to be some of your best friends in your adult life.
—*Age 25*

I've learned that when I want something done around my house, all I have to do is mention to my dad that I'm going to do it myself. —*Age 37*

I've learned that you leave a little piece of yourself with everyone you teach. —*Age 26*

I've learned that a good-looking doctor can make your blood pressure go up. —*Age 43*

I've learned that it's no fun putting on a wet swimsuit.

—Age 29

I've learned that saving is just like dieting: It's never too late to start.

—Age 33

I've learned that if you're too embarrassed to tell your best friend about something you've done, then you shouldn't have done it in the first place.

—Age 25

I've learned that it's not what you have in your life but who you have in your life that counts.

—*Age 30*

I've learned that traffic lights and golf balls never do what you tell them to, no matter how much you shout at them.

—*Age 43*

I've learned that when a girl keeps on teasing you and says she doesn't like you and bugs you all the time, she really likes you.

—*Age 8*

I've learned that my car runs better going home.

—*Age 92*

I've learned that no matter how hard you try, you can't get ice out of the freezer without dropping at least one cube.

—*Age 32*

I've learned that I'm the special person I've been saving the good dishes for.

—*Age 61*

I've learned that two people can look at the same exact thing and see something totally different.

—*Age 20*

I've learned that when you say "I'm not supposed
to tell you this but . . .," you've said too much
already.

—*Age 19*

I've learned that giving flowers makes me just as
happy as receiving them.

—*Age 23*

I've learned that a little dog hair never hurt
anybody.

—*Age 79*

I've learned that if you want peace and quiet, don't buy your four-year-old a whistle—no matter how much he begs.　　　　　　　　—*Age 43*

I've learned that if you can't fit it in a van, you probably can't fit it in a dorm room.　　　—*Age 18*

I've learned that there are only two classes: first class and no class.　　　　　　　　　　—*Age 20*

I've learned that you should never tell your four-teen-year-old brother you can beat him up unless you're sure you can.
—*Age 21*

I've learned that if you want to know if you love someone, watch them when they're asleep. —*Age 46*

I've learned that imagining God standing beside me stops me from doing things I know are wrong.
—*Age 15*

I've learned that my hair will be perfect on nights
I'm home alone and unmanageable when I have a
date.   —*Age 20*

I've learned that it's not a good idea to put bubble
bath in a Jacuzzi.   —*Age 32*

*I've learned that it's a good marriage when both
mates think they got better than they deserve.* —*Age 43*

I've learned that before you make fun of a certain car, make sure your boyfriend's parents don't own one.

—Age 19

I've learned that you're not always perfect on the first try.

—Age 10

I've learned that the teachings and example of my parents are as valuable as a college education.

—Age 20

I've learned that the "speedy service" signs at fast-food drive-through windows are there to make you laugh.

—Age 31

I've learned that you can't be too old to hold your father's hand.

—Age 11

I've learned that I shouldn't keep dating my boyfriend just because he's good at fixing my car.

—Age 23

I've learned that when there's something unpleasant to do, do it first.　　　*—Age 79*

I've learned that all cars lose their new car smell no matter how much they cost.　　　*—Age 29*

I've learned that what makes me happiest is my son holding my face in his hands and telling me I'm the best mom he could ever have.　　　*—Age 48*

I've learned that there should be an Eleventh Commandment — Thou shalt not whine.

—Age 62

I've learned that the biggest regrets in life are the chances you never take.
—*Age 17*

I've learned that when your children first get their driver's licenses, you are willing to drive them anywhere.
—*Age 56*

I've learned that you should never count your money while sitting in a moving car with the windows open.
—*Age 27*

I've learned that you don't have to keep running after you've caught the bus.
—*Age 20*

I've learned that in old age you spend half your time looking for a bathroom and the other half trying to remember people's names.
—*Age 65*

I've learned that I know there are angels around me protecting me, but sometimes I feel as if they're off duty.
—*Age 12*

I've learned that it's better to invite guests on a rainy day as dust doesn't show as much as when it is sunny.
—*Age 65*

I've learned that every day we are offered twice as many opportunities as misfortunes.
—*Age 33*

I've learned that to save yourself the price of a face-lift, smile a lot.
—*Age 55*

I've learned that the best answer my mother gave me as a child was "because I'm the mom, that's why."

- —Age 25

I've learned that you should never leave home without a sense of humor.

—Age 69

I've learned that by the time I can afford it, I don't want it anymore.

—Age 56

I've learned that you're never too old to be tucked in.
—Age 19

I've learned that the panicky feeling you get when your purse is missing is difficult to surpass. *—Age 62*

I've learned that sometimes watching a child fail is the most painful but necessary thing a parent can endure.
—Age 48

I've learned that simple truths remain and the things that matter most rarely ever change. —*Age 56*

I've learned that you should never let your four-year-old brother cut your hair. —*Age 11*

I've learned that self-discipline, courage, and good character are impregnable to the assaults of bad luck. —*Age 47*

I've learned that whoever said you can't buy happiness forgot about puppies. —*Age 28*

I've learned that children stop being children, but you never stop being their mother. —*Age 38*

I've learned that I shouldn't waste my weekends by worrying about what faces me in the office on Monday. —*Age 28*

I've learned that wisdom is not how much you know but how you use what you know.   —*Age 57*

I've learned that nothing is impossible for the man who doesn't have to do it himself.   —*Age 22*

I've learned that you should never blow a big bubble with your gum if your head is out the window of a car going 40 mph and you have long hair.

—*Age 18*

I've learned that grandmothers hate washing off those little fingerprints left by the precious little hands of their grandchildren. —*Age 65*

I've learned that Thursdays are "yes" days. People are more open and relaxed and more favorable on Thursdays. —*Age 39*

I've learned that no one is too old for a water gun fight. —*Age 19*

I've learned
that a best
friend is some-
one who loves
you when you
forget to love
yourself.

—Age 18

I've learned that the slowest lane of traffic is
always the one I'm in. —*Age 42*

I've learned that peeing in the woods with a
couple of friends can be a real bonding
experience. —*Age 20*

I've learned that no matter what time you decide
to go to the bank, everyone else has decided to go
then, too. —*Age 28*

I've learned that when you're looking for something, it's usually the last one in the pile.   —*Age 27*

I've learned that there is a very crucial difference between charm and character.   —*Age 37*

I've learned that sometimes the things that scare you the most turn out to be the best times of your life.   —*Age 20*

I've learned that to really understand how much my father loves me, I needed to have a son. —*Age 30*

I've learned that everything I truly value has been gained by vulnerability on my part. It is the secret to life.

—*Age 21*

I've learned that just because you've gotten in the last word doesn't mean you've won the argument.

—*Age 61*

I've learned that my mom smells better when she
doesn't have perfume on.   —*Age 10*

I've learned that I'd rather have a lot of brothers
and sisters and not get many things than have no
brothers and sisters and get everything.   —*Age 13*

I've learned that once you retire and draw social
security, everything you have either hurts or
doesn't work.   —*Age 66*

I've learned that no matter how busy someone is, they're never too busy to tell you how busy they are.
—Age 42

I've learned that it's just as important to be friendly to the janitor as it is to be friendly to the company president.
—Age 23

I've learned that when I'm alone in my room, I have a beautiful singing voice.
—Age 16

I've learned that if the peanut butter and jelly don't leak out of the sandwich, there's not enough peanut butter and jelly on it. —Age 50

I've learned that trying to smile while saying "soy sauce" will always make you laugh. —Age 20

I've learned that if you want an honest answer about how you look, ask your little sister. —Age 13

I've learned that a good friend is better than a therapist.

—*Age 19*

I've learned that sandwiches cut diagonally taste better.
—*Age 38*

I've learned that God doesn't ask you to be the best, just to do your best.
—*Age 25*

I've learned as a lifeguard that when you throw nickels in the pool without anyone seeing you, it brings many smiles to the children who find them.
—*Age 19*

I've learned that you never, ever wear an over-priced bridesmaid dress again to another event no matter what the bride tells you. —*Age 28*

I've learned that kids will pretty much meet the expectations that you set for them. —*Age 38*

I've learned that nothing ruins a marriage or relationship as much as the constant use of the word *mine*. —*Age 66*

I've learned that when asking a child what he's up to, never believe the reply "Nothing."   —*Age 20*

I've learned that arguing with a teenager is like mud wrestling a pig; you both get dirty and the pig loves it.   —*Age 48*

I've learned that I should never go into my parents' bedroom on Sunday nights.   —*Age 13*

I've learned that learning to laugh at yourself is the
surest sign of maturity.   *—Age 47*

I've learned that you should never cut or highlight
your own hair.   *—Age 28*

I've learned that you should never leave a seven-
year-old with a bat and ball alone by a window
while baby-sitting him.   *—Age 13*

I've learned that sometimes you should just let your heart decide and deal with reality later. —*Age 21*

I've learned that God gives you a new gift every day.
—*Age 7*

I've learned that you should thank the salesclerks who take the time to compare the signature on your credit card with the signature on the receipt.

—*Age 24*

I've learned that going to the doctor's office is like going to church. You don't want to be late, but you don't want to get there too early either. —*Age 37*

I've learned that when my dad says he's going to barbecue, it means we're going to have a burned piece of meat for supper. —*Age 13*

I've learned that if you hang something in a closet for a while it shrinks two sizes. —*Age 62*

I've learned that when your children complain about doing household chores, you simply tell them that they are either tenants or family members. If they're tenants, they pay rent; if they're family members, they assume responsibilities. —*Age 48*

I've learned that moms make mistakes too. —*Age 16*

I've learned that worry's best antidote is action.

—*Age 55*

I've learned that "yuck" is not the best response when your mom tells you what's for dinner.

—*Age 12*

I've learned that peer pressure is just too much;
when I'm alone I'm a completely different person
than I am at school.
—Age 12

I've learned that you're never too old for slumber
parties.
—Age 19

I've learned that the only thing you do your first
year of college is to gain weight. Then you spend
the next three years trying to lose it.
—Age 20

I've learned that love isn't something you look for, it's something you give. —*Age 36*

I've learned that in twenty years no one is going to care about what I got on my biology final. —*Age 16*

I've learned that no matter how many clothes I iron the night before, I will end up wearing something else. —*Age 28*

I've learned that the way you speak of your husband to others either builds up your family or casts a cloud over it.   — *Age 58*

I've learned that you should never take sides when your friends are upset with each other.   —*Age 13*

I've learned that you can't give a hug without getting one in return.   —*Age 36*

I've learned that young women tend to marry men who know how to make them laugh. —*Age 53*

I've learned that life is full of good surprises even if they do seem to come far apart. —*Age 58*

I've learned that a great picker-upper is when I hear my grandchild say, "Come sit by me, Grandma." —*Age 60*

I've learned that whenever I get mad at my mom,
I should try to remember that she loves me. —*Age 10*

*I've learned that dreams are where you want to go;
work is how you get there.*   —*Age 20*

I've learned that you can't make friends by waiting
for other people to step forward. You need to
make the first move.   —*Age 14*

I've learned that the question parents hate the most is "Why?"

—*Age 15*

I've learned that the fastest way to get a green light is to start writing something down while you're at a red light.

—*Age 42*

I've learned that when your wife asks for a kiss, you shouldn't say, "I already did."

—*Age 67*

I've learned that chocolate is a food group.

—*Age 55*

I've learned that you should never put a rubber snake in your older brother's bed.
—*Age 7*

I've learned that getting fired can be the best thing to ever happen.
—*Age 32*

I've learned that all your school pictures look good except the one in the yearbook that everyone sees forever.
—*Age 14*

I've learned that what people want most in life is to be loved and appreciated.

—*Age 21*

I've learned that my piano teacher gets a funny look on her face when she notices I haven't practiced.

—*Age 11*

I've learned that you cannot make someone love you. All you can do is be someone who can be loved. After that, it's up to them.

—*Age 51*

I've learned that you should never teach your little brothers how to use a slingshot.
—*Age 13*

I've learned that it's a good idea to ask for the details before you say yes when someone asks, "Can you do me a small favor?"
—*Age 37*

I've learned that praying for your enemies instead of fighting with them helps both them and you. —*Age 14*

I've learned that you spend the first year of your children's lives trying to get them to walk and talk, then the rest of your life trying to get them to sit down and shut up.
—*Age 41*

I've learned that planning a vacation is sometimes just as much fun as experiencing it.
—*Age 48*

I've learned that my father lets me do things my mother would never even think about.
—*Age 13*

I've learned that parents always bring up those embarrassing childhood stories at all the wrong moments.

—Age 15

I've learned that a dropped screw or nail in the garage becomes instantly invisible.

—Age 60

I've learned that there is no greater feeling of self-worth than when you help someone in need.

—Age 27

I've learned that receiving a thoughtful note or unexpected act of kindness from someone can make my day.   —*Age 18*

I've learned that while it's important to be my daughter's friend, it's more important to be her mother.   —*Age 35*

I've learned that it's possible to fall madly in love with just one glance.   —*Age 21*

I've learned that it's the teacher and not
the subject that makes a class interesting.

—*Age 23*

I've learned that you shouldn't talk about what you're going to do. Do it, then talk.   —*Age 49*

I've learned that nothing is better than coming home to a lit fireplace on a cold, snowy night and drinking hot chocolate.   —*Age 19*

I've learned that competing with a friend over a man is a fun game unless one of you actually wins.

—*Age 21*

I've learned that having a boss who makes you sick isn't a terminal condition.

—Age 47

I've learned that adolescence is a time of growing and experiencing. I just didn't know it would hurt so much.

—Age 15

I've learned that because my parents believe in me, I believe in me.

—Age 23

I've learned that your children can make you happier or madder than you've ever been in your life. —*Age 32*

I've learned that when you take your girlfriend out for lunch and she orders the salad bar because she's on a diet, before the lunch is over, she'll eat half of your cheese fries. —*Age 46*

I've learned that onion breath isn't bad when your spouse has it too. —*Age 32*

I've learned that when you go somewhere and they say "Don't bring valuables," DON'T BRING VALUABLES!

—Age 12

I've learned that when a woman says she's not mad, she usually is.

—Age 24

I've learned that it is fun when my mom lets me carve my initials in a new jar of peanut butter.

—Age 16

I've learned that I get in trouble if I lick a lollipop, let my dog lick it, and then lick it again.   —*Age 8*

I've learned that it's easy to be critical about something you've never experienced.   —*Age 51*

I've learned that I'm glad I grew up in a poor household. It taught me that one doesn't need a lot of money to be happy and that there's an advantage to having to struggle a bit.   —*Age 23*

I've learned that having extra time to spend with my children is more important than having extra money to spend on them. —*Age 34*

I've learned that when you love someone, you see with your heart instead of your eyes. —*Age 13*

I've learned that any cheap brownie mix can be good when chocolate chips are added to the batter.

—*Age 34*

I've learned that you should never fall in love at summer camp. It ends, but life goes on. —*Age 17*

I've learned that when the duties of being a teacher overwhelm me, my students almost always brighten my day in some small way. —*Age 39*

I've learned that it scares me to walk in the bathroom and see my grandpa's teeth on the sink.

—*Age 16*

I've learned that the copy machine
can tell when I'm in a hurry.

—Age 20

I've learned that excellent service from someone deserves a letter written to that person's boss and a request that the letter be placed in the employee's personnel file.

—*Age 31*

I've learned that money talks but all mine ever says is, "Good-bye."

—*Age 13*

I've learned that you always gain five pounds on the scale at the doctor's office.

—*Age 12*

I've learned that "You look great" is not sexual harassment. —*Age 32*

I've learned that you shouldn't write the name of whom you love really big on your new backpack that you have to wear to school everyday. —*Age 12*

I've learned that college isn't just about preparing for your future career, it is about finding out who you are right now. —*Age 23*

I've learned that the sticky price tags on items purchased at a discount store are always harder to remove than the price tags on items purchased at a prestigious store.
—*Age 33*

I've learned that if you can laugh at yourself, you will always be amused.
—*Age 31*

I've learned that I love being a senior; it's graduation I'm worried about.
—*Age 79*

I've learned that when a society accepts the premise that individuals are not responsible for their own actions, it's in real trouble. —*Age 71*

I've learned that no matter what mood I'm in, James Taylor is always perfect. —*Age 19*

I've learned that life is like a book. Sometimes we must close a chapter and begin the next one. —*Age 34*

I've learned that it's hard to determine where to draw the line between being nice and not hurting people's feelings and standing up for what you believe.
—Age 12

I've learned that you know you're in love when you don't have to ask anyone else if you are. *—Age 20*

I've learned that giving doesn't count if you don't want what you're giving away.
—Age 11

I've learned that when you're worried, give your
troubles to God; He will be up all night anyway.

—*Age 47*

I've learned that wherever I go, I should try to
leave it either cleaner or happier than it was before
I arrived.

—*Age 19*

*I've learned that if Mom's on a diet, everyone's on
a diet.*

—*Age 10*

I've learned that within each person is a treasure, but sometimes you have to dig for it.   —*Age 32*

I've learned that success is having money to pay the bills and still have enough to order a pizza without a coupon.   —*Age 47*

I've learned that there are two places you are always welcome: church and Grandma's house.

—*Age 12*

Dear Reader,

If life has taught you a thing or two and you would like to pass it on, please mail it to me with your name, age, and address. I would welcome the opportunity of sharing it with other readers in a future book. Thank you.

H. Jackson Brown, Jr.
P.O. Box 150014
Nashville, TN 37215